Look Out!

Ruby Lee
Art by Heather Jacolbia

Literacy Consultants
David Booth • Kathleen Corrigan

Look out!

Here comes a scooter.

Look out!

Here comes a car.

Look out!

Here comes a van.

Look out!

Here comes a bus.

Look out!

Here comes a truck.

Look out!

Here comes a fire truck.

Look out!

Here we come!